LINES FOR ALL OCCASIONS

Sweet Nothings & Pillow Talk

KNOCK KNOCK®
VENICE, CALIFORNIA

Created and published by Knock Knock
Distributed by Who's There Inc.
Venice, CA 90291
knockknockstuff.com

ISBN: 978-160106668-8
UPC: 825703-50118-6

10 9 8 7 6 5 4 3 2 1

Contents

You had me at "I'll clean the bathroom."

Introduction

PREPARING TO START THE SMOOTH TALK

We have a basic human need to connect with others. From an evolutionary perspective, we first created social bonds as a survival tactic, huddling together for warmth, uttering our first words to signal fear or celebrate the discovery of food. To be alone in prehistoric times was to invite a tragic fate. Somewhere in the distant past, however, humans developed to the point where they no longer needed *everyone* in the tribe to stay alive. They could play favorites—deciding which fellow hominid they would share a choice hunk of roast antelope with simply because they *liked* them more than the others. Still, if delivering meat was the only way early man could say "I just called to say I love you," the development of speech was a huge evolutionary leap in convenience alone. And thus was born the romantic gesture we now call the sweet nothing: the sly, antediluvian art of enticing another to "come up and see me sometime."

If you are one of the tens of millions of singles circulating in the vast and turbulent dating pool looking to do a little human bonding—or if you're currently in an amorous relationship and seeking to keep it fresh and fulfilling—gentle sweet nothings are your ultimate wingmen. This is the way we were meant to evolve: into higher-thinking beings comfortable with pillow-talking our way to sealing the deal. To be tongue-tied in the modern world is to risk the contemporary equivalent of death by wooly mammoth stampede. Thankfully, you hold in your hands a hardbound lexicon of rapier quips, which permits even the most socially inept *Homo sapiens* to survive on the battlefield of love.

Current online dating data shows that what's most important in dating is not a row of perfectly white teeth, a set of chiseled abs, nor even a bulging checkbook, it is having common interests and a good personality that scores highest with prospective mates. Put simply, words matter. And not just any words, but meaningful, intimate ones that demonstrate you understand your beloved. "Verbal intimacy," described by the relationship experts at dating website eHarmony as "the most important indicator of whether a person is right for you," isn't mere woo-woo mumbo jumbo. According to relationship expert and author Georgianna Donadio, PhD, it's an actual scientific fact. "The best time to share your feelings," she explains explicitly, "is just before or during sex. At that time, levels of oxytocin, a hormone that enhances feelings of trust, love and intimacy, are elevated, making it the very best moment to love talk with your partner."

We may have long ago swapped our damp caves for glass towers, but seduction is a game we continue to play. Back then it was about the survival of the species. Today, it's only slightly less crucial. In our high-tech, hyper-lingual society, hunting and gathering prowess or a talent for nitpicking simply aren't as prized as the skills of a superior sweet-talker. If we are to gain that all-important human contact, we must acquire the verbal mastery that can attract, pursue, cajole, and, most importantly, keep loved ones close by our side. In other words, fancy pillow talk is the new gift of roast antelope. Isn't it time you brought home the bacon?

SEXY SEX

When you just want to bow-chicka-wow-wow

SURE, WE HUMANS MAY BE HIGH-
functioning animals capable of
such complex skills as making
fire, reading, and program-
ming the garage door opener.
Yet animals we remain, and as
such we have animalistic needs.
First there is food—then there
is sex (followed closely by sleep,
which often occurs directly
after sex—imagine that).

Her 2.0

In 2010, inventor Douglas Hines created
Roxxxy, the talking female sex robot. Roxxxy
comes with several preprogrammed personali-
ties—S&M Susan, Frigid Farah, and more—
and can even learn your likes and dislikes.
If that sounds like the end is nigh, don't tell
futurist Ian Yeoman and sexologist Michelle
Mars from New Zealand's Victoria University.
They predict robot prostitutes will be ready,
willing, and saying all the right things by 2050.

Humans, in search of carnal sat-
isfaction, must resign themselves
to wooing other humans. The
problem is, pitching said woo
is a complex, time-consuming
endeavor. And let's be honest—
sometimes you just want to
cut to the chase and get *busy.*

Hunters and gatherers advanced
their search for sustenance by

developing farming. As for the quest for copulation, there is no better (legal) method of enticing a mate than to employ the power of speech—in other words, to *charm the pants off them.*

That is where this chapter comes in. With these lines, you are assured of a quick and dirty seduction strike. The following pages are the verbal version of a peacock's feathers—colorful and mesmerizing for maximum per-suasion. Plus, they prove you have brains to complement your beauty and/or brawn. Because even if all you're after is a knuckle-dragging booty call, it helps to demon-strate from the get-go that you are capable of doing more with your mouth than mere breathing.

Man to Woman

The junk in your trunk
would be worth a lot on
Antiques Roadshow.

———•◦•———

This place might not get the
Dodgers channel, but I'm
about to get to third base.

———•◦•———

Have I showed you
my power tool?

———•◦•———

Of course I'm a feminist. I love
when a girl's in charge.

———•◦•———

I can last all night without
a plug or batteries.

———•◦•———

Whenever a woman meets me,
she starts hearing Barry White
music in her head.

Have you noticed
the size of my feet?

———•—•———

Some would say a woman like
you is hard to come by. Let me
show you why I'd disagree.

———•—•———

Do you prefer clever flirtation
or blatant begging?

———•—•———

Your skin would look great
against my sheets.

———•—•———

I have a new screwdriver.
Wanna come over and show
me how to use it?

———•—•———

I'm not a yes man. More of
a "yes, yes, YES" man.

If you're trying to get a rise
out of me, it's working.

You look like you don't have a mean
bone in your body. Would you like one?

Woman to Man

Be Mr. Right to my Ms. Now.

My daddy warned me about boys like
you . . . good thing he's not here.

Do you have a license for those guns?

In case you didn't notice, my
boobs are down here.

My porn star name is Velvet
Cherry. What's yours?

I'm too much for one man.
Have you got a brother?

———•·•———

I've got gin. When can I come
by and get some of your juice?

———•·•———

I'm a vegetarian, but you could
probably coax me back to meat.

I'll Have What She's Having

Here's a sweet-talk safety tip: use your inside
voice. In 2009, Caroline Cartwright was pulled
before a UK magistrate for ignoring a previ-
ous "anti-social behavior" order for sexual
noises described as "murder" and "unnatural."
Neighbors, the postman, and a woman walking
by with her child all complained. Her next-door
neighbor said, "The noise sounds like they are
both in considerable pain. I cannot describe the
noise. I have never ever heard anything like it."

Could Go Both Ways

C'mon now, that bed's not
going to unmake itself.

Let's put the "us" in lust.

Is it hot in here, or is that
your red-hot aura?

Birds do it, bees do it, let's
do it . . . let's have sex.

Want to see my other tattoos?

I believe the DJ's playing our
song: "Let's Get It On."

Wanna find out how
many times you can thank
God before passing out?

I don't know how
to spell ecstasy, but
I know how to make it.

———•—•———

Can I see the notches
on your bedpost?

———•—•———

Bring along a fire hose 'cause
I'm smokin' in bed.

———•—•———

How many drinks will it
take for you to like me?

———•—•———

That's quite a vocabulary you have.
What other big words do you know?

———•—•———

Every room's a steam room
when you walk in.

———•—•———

Want to be my soul mate
for a couple of hours?

Tip: Sexting for Grownups

Sexting: teenagers shouldn't do it, but adults should, if they want to charge up their sex lives. Surveys have shown that many adults are already sexting. Therapist Esther Perel thinks sexting is great foreplay, a "creative intervention for couples trying to rekindle their relationships." Even AARP joined the conversation, noting that sexting is a great way to express yourself when you're shy about whispering sweet nothings face to face.

Can you come over and
play on my swing?

I can't help but notice that your
spirit animal is humping my leg.

Are you speaking French, or is that
just wishful thinking on my part?

Let me not to the marriage of
true minds admit impediments,
'cause I want to get with you.

I gave up one-night stands for Lent,
but I'm not a very good Catholic.

Someone call Isaac Newton—you're
defying the laws of gravity.

I may not be religious, but I
do speak in tongues.

Shall we retire to your boudoir and
make the beast with two backs?

I hear you've got an Olympic
gold medal in toe curling.

My bedside manner is great, but
my in-bed manner is even better.

Adulterous

You're exactly what I've been
looking for—minus the ring.

———•———

What my husband doesn't
know should please you.

———•———

I can't imagine anyone else I'd
rather sneak around behind my
wife's back with than you.

———•———

I cherish your confidentiality most of all.

———•———

Why don't you slip off that
ring and get comfortable?

———•———

Being with you makes me
want to get a divorce.

———•———

You're the mistress every
married man is looking for.

Ours is truly an affair to remember.

We just committed enough cardinal
sins for a papal conclave.

No Shame

Your body is a temple, and I'd
love to be your congregation.

Dangle that dessert in my face
and I'll eat all the frosting.

I hope our fairy tale has a happy ending.

Let's make like a hammer and
nails and get to bangin'.

Forget pillow talk. Let's
go for pillow scream.

I ought to wash your mouth out with soap, especially after where it's been.

———•———

You look great in those jeans, but my genes would look even better in you.

———•———

I see the rumors are true—dildo models really do exist.

———•———

I only eat organic. Lucky thing you only dye the hair on your head.

———•———

Do you know what'd look good on you? Me.

———•———

Your friend said you're kind of pervy. I hope it's true.

———•———

You had me at "hello, let's screw."

———•———

You'd go down like a single malt scotch.

I say we hit that hot dog and donut
shop hard—it's open all night.

———————

I have my own big bang theory
I'd like to test out.

———————

I'll let you pay for dinner if
you let me put in the tip.

What Do Men Want?

Thanks to a recent study about Valentine's Day
by researchers at ScienceofRelationships.com,
we now know that while "men hate it more than
women do," it doesn't mean they're immune
to the amorous gesture—they just think of intimacy in more practical terms. Where women
see the holiday as an opportunity to receive
love and affection, men want more useful
things like massages, sensual products, and
"better than average sex." Imagine that.

COURTSHIP

When someone has caught your eye

If pickup lines are all about raw, carnal lust, courtship speaks to the higher, spiritual call of love. Any modern-day Casanova might look to "How YOU doin'?" or "What's your sign?" as classic statements of thoughtful introduction. In contrast, the courtier looks to John Cusack's boom box serenade or Jerry Maguire's "You complete me" as the statements to beat. To court is to place class over simplistic craving—

Be a Saint

Showering one's sweetie with chocolate-covered goodies may make Valentine's Day a costly holiday, but be thankful we're not living in ancient Rome. The holiday traces its origin back to the feast of Lupercalia, a three-day festival where single men would beat single women with the skins of sacrificed dogs and goats, a practice believed to promote fertility. Couples were partnered by lottery—and apparently were expected to fornicate for the length of the festival.

but for those without Oscar-caliber skills of expression, the challenge is to make an honest, heartfelt statement without sounding hopelessly wan and old-fashioned.

Perhaps the greatest misconception about courtship is that one must become one's worst saccharine self. This is sheer nonsense. Just ask

Lord Byron. Love poems written by the "mad, bad, and dangerous to know" English poet are powerful, epic declarations that inspire ardent action. Indeed, Byron's signature move is the grand gesture. And so it is in the way of courtship: it is to be gallant, passionate, and when playing—one plays for keeps.

Lest you think a Byronesque posture may only be adopted in service of life-changing moments such as a marriage proposal, think again. Unleashing a subtle, yet overtly romantic statement on a first date has an uncanny way of demonstrating you live without fear of failure or rejection. Rather than tossing out a throwaway line unintended to be taken seriously, try whispering a "sweet something" from this chapter and feel your gravitas surge.

The Romantic

Those are lips I could kiss
for the rest of my life.

———————

Michelangelo couldn't have carved
anything more beautiful than you.

———————

Only fools fall in love—and nothing
makes me feel more foolish than you.

———————

Now I know why love
songs were invented.

———————

If we were in a movie right now,
I'd be John Cusack outside your
window holding up a radio.

———————

I hope I can see you again, someplace
other than my dreams.

———————

Romeo and Juliet have nothing on us.

If we ever broke up, you'd be
the one that got away.

———•◦•———

May I worship you from a-near?

———•◦•———

I should get a second career as
your stunt double, because I'm
obviously falling for you.

———•◦•———

I'd buy you a drink but I'd
get jealous of the glass.

———•◦•———

I'm very articulate when
you're not around.

———•◦•———

Good thing my phone has GPS,
because I'm lost in your eyes.

———•◦•———

Didn't we meet in one of
my dreams last week?

———•◦•———

Now I know what love is.

The Flatterer

Do you insure your legs?

———•—•———

You've got more fabulous
than a drag queen.

———•—•———

If I knew my blind date
was going to be this hot,
I would have worn sunscreen.

———•—•———

If we were on *The Bachelor*, I'd
give you the final rose.

———•—•———

You smell like cherry pie.

———•—•———

I bet our kids will be
beautiful with your eyes.

———•—•———

You can't expect me to believe
you *don't* have a fan club.

You're the first person I've
dated my dog likes.

You are the greatest thing
since beer in cans.

I've never seen
someone as attractive as you
who wasn't on film.

Tip: So Snoutfair

Spice up your vocabulary with a trip into the distant past—when "snoutfair" meant handsome, an alluring woman was said to be "illecebrous," and a man might "cast a sheep's eye" (look amorously) upon his sweetheart in the manner thusly: *"Greetings, my wonder-wench!"* Use such obsolete words with a minimum of "bobance" (arrogance), dear reader. Heard by the wrong ears, such language may cause a most "lungeous pussyvan" (irritable temper) to erupt.

I can't wait for the day your
laugh starts to annoy me.

———•———

The weird way you put on your
shirt is incredibly cute.

———•———

The timbre of your voice
excites my ears.

———•———

Even the way you walk is endearing.

The Commitment-Ready

You'd look great in a tux . . .
and standing at the altar.

———•———

Can you imagine what our grandkids
will say about this first date?

———•———

I can't promise you the moon,
but I might be able to come
through with Mars and Venus.

Can I be the last person on
Earth that you go out with?

———•—•———

Will you plant a garden with me?

———•—•———

If we have kids together, I'll always be
the one to take them to porta-potties.

———•—•———

Marry me, and you'll never have to
scratch your own itches again.

———•—•———

If you're not in love with me
now, it's only a matter of time.

———•—•———

I want a lifetime of your
morning bedhead.

———•—•———

Come live with me and be my love,
and we will binge-watch
Netflix together.

This is Your Brain on Love

If the mere sight of the one you love gives you sweats and causes your pulse to quicken, you have the ventral tegmental area of your brain to thank. This tiny crumb of gray matter is responsible for releasing both the stress hormone norepinephrine as well as the pleasure-inducing neurotransmitter dopamine—making love's potent effect on the body approaching something close to that of meth. Crazy in love, indeed!

My mom will make a great mother-in-law.

———•———

I'd give up Grindr for you.

———•———

I'd eat kale for you.

———•———

I'd send your mother Mother's Day cards every year if you fell for me.

I can't imagine ever wanting
anyone but you.

———•◦•———

I can't wait to meet your parents!

———•◦•———

I could get used to all these fireworks.

———•◦•———

Your body is a wonderland. And
I just swallowed the red pill.

———•◦•———

We're gonna need a bigger bed.

———•◦•———

I can't quit you.

———•◦•———

Where have you been all my life?

———•◦•———

With you, suddenly every
day is Valentine's Day.

———•◦•———

And . . . cue the confetti!

The Suave & Confident

I thank the gods of Groupon for landing
us in these same ten yoga classes.

Just curious, but what's your ring size?

You are living proof God really
does run a modeling agency.

Everyone's got their thing. In our case,
that thing would be perfection.

Can I take you off the market?

You can stop looking.
You've found me.

Do you believe in fate?
Because it clearly believes in me.

I was just asking Santa for
someone like you.

———•◦•———

My NCAA bracket's got you and me
closing out the dance, baby.

———•◦•———

There's Anthony & Cleopatra,
Romeo & Juliet, and then
there's You & Me.

———•◦•———

I won't ever ask you to have a
threesome with your best friend.

———•◦•———

I would never call your father an
overbearing pompous asshole
if we got married.

———•◦•———

I'd pretend to go do volunteer work
if you went out with me.

———•◦•———

I'd even eat cow brains if you'd
go to dinner with me.

The Dork, the Nerd, & the Geek

You're like Jessica Rabbit and HAL
9000 rolled into one: hot and calculating.

———

You've cast a powerful
spell on me, m'lady.

———

You may wield my magic sword any day.

———

You're the Ryan Gosling of
my little Hobbiton.

———

You've earned the high score
at my heart arcade.

———

You're my greatest non-fantasy
role-playing fantasy girl.

———

You couldn't be more perfect
for me if I purchased you on
a Japanese anime website.

I knew our avatars would get along.

At last, a nerd who really
gets my dork side.

You make me feel like the only
girl at a sci-fi convention.

I'm a closet superhero—
want to be my trusty sidekick?

The Cheerleader Effect

While courting your next mate, know that you
may seem more attractive if you hang out with
a few same-sex pals. Researchers at the University
of California, San Diego, showed that
one tends to "average out" the look of faces
when observing a group, and average faces
are considered aesthetically pleasing. Sorry,
unique beauties—surround yourself with more
average-looking people if you'd like to offset
your offbeat (and potentially off-putting) looks.

The Manipulator

If anyone can heal my heart,
it's you.

———•———

I love it when you say loving things.

———•———

Being with you makes me feel so safe,
like I can be completely vulnerable.

———•———

I'll never say yes, no matter
how many times you ask me
if you "look fat in these."

———•———

I'd fight Satan for your garbage.

———•———

Let's have dinner with your parents—
I love it when we all hang out.

———•———

You can't do any better than me.

I trust you so much I want to give
you my passwords—you probably
want to do the same, right?

———•———

I'll miss you so much when I'm gone—
I want to spend every minute together.
Can you give me a ride to the airport?

———•———

I'll even love you when
you're old and wrinkly.

———•———

You can make up
for my lack of money with
your sense of humor.

———•———

Before you, I'd never
wanted anyone to talk to me
for hours on end like that.

———•———

You weren't easy. I prefer to
think of you as less difficult.

RELATIONSHIPS

When things start to get real

LONG-LASTING RELATIONSHIPS
are not uncommon in the animal
world. For instance, over 90 percent
of bird species are monogamous.
But considering the average life
span of a bird is well under
twenty years, one may assume
most birds simply don't live long
enough to get bored with their
mates. Nature's lesson to long-
living humans is clear: happy

What I Did For Love

Henry Blum and Emmania Rodriguez met in 2004 in a video arcade thanks to their mutual passion for Dance Dance Revolution. Initially, Henry's fast feet were too much for Emmania, but he always knew she was the dance partner of his dreams. Years later, he surprised her by installing one of the arcade machines in their basement, getting down on one knee and asking, "Will you be my player two for life?" Eight months later, they were married.

relationships depend on creativity. And so, cue the pillow talk.

In modern bonding, the culprit is often daily routine: make breakfast, rush to work, pay bills, fold laundry, rinse, repeat. There's nothing shameful in acknowledging that couples require tiny shocks to keep life's rhythms from becoming numbing patterns. You may consider the charming, coyly sensual lines within this chapter as small, shocking gestures to awaken the dormant libido. In fact, you may find it most useful to insert a clever line or two into an otherwise tedious everyday chore. Imagine converting the unpacking of groceries into a vegetable-strewn voyage of tabletop passion? Before you grow old, or even if you already are, it's not too late to practice giving any ordinary task that extra *oomph.*

Whether you're keeping the flame alive, rekindling the romance, or struggling to recall the reasons you got together in the first place—remember: it's the little things, or the sweet nothings, that show you (still) care.

Moving In Together

We can get rid of all my weird furniture.

I'm really good at playing house.

Wanna mingle our undies?

You can warm your hands on
me anytime—even if it makes
me squeal like a little girl.

I love you so much I don't care
that you take up nine-tenths
of the bed every night.

If we were peasants,
I'd always sleep on the drafty
side of the hay pile.

Would you fill my bathroom
with your products?

Would you come take up more than
your fair share of closet space?

I can't wait to come home and find
you sitting in my favorite chair.

Even when you have morning
breath, you're the first thing I want
to smell every morning.

I love you even though I smash
my knee when I get in the car
because you never move the seat back.

Buttering Up

My lips never get tired of kissing you.

All your sweet nothings mean
something to me.

I didn't just fall in love with you,
it was a complete face plant.

———·———

With a wife like you, every night
is like date night.

———·———

You really are my partner in crime,
because you always steal my heart.

———·———

Are you a race car driver?
Because you went from girlfriend
to wife in no time.

———·———

Every minute with you is like
a lifetime in paradise.

———·———

Do you get tired of being
right all the time?

———·———

Why go out? Everyone I need is here.

———·———

Those pants look perfect on you.

Daily Life: Kitchen

How about tonight I can do the
dishes, and you can do me?

———

A day without you is like forgetting to
take out the garbage—it just stinks.

———

I was just stuffing large gherkins in a
tight pickle jar and thought of you.

Give It a Shot

Science may have found a cure for the unfaith-
ful lover, thanks to our tiny rodent friend the
vole. It seems one type of vole is monogamous,
while another is a rampant philanderer. But
when researchers injected the cheater voles
with a neurochemical combo of oxytocin and
vasopressin, the furry little cads abandoned
their debauched ways and stuck with their
long-term mates. So . . . if monogamy is just an
injection away, will health insurance cover it?

Let's skip dinner and get right to dessert.

———•◦•———

I'll give you another reason to
clear the table right now.

———•◦•———

You can have the last bite of pie.

———•◦•———

You'd look hotter in the rubber gloves
if you didn't wear anything else.

———•◦•———

I'm thinking of toasting some
buns—bring those over here.

———•◦•———

I'm a locavore—I only eat
things found in my kitchen.

———•◦•———

I've always thought sausage and
clam makes a great étouffée.

———•◦•———

It's called butcher block because
it's where I like to put the meat.

I always prefer my tacos soft.

—•—

In my kitchen, melons are
always in season.

—•—

The sink isn't the only thing
that's wet in this kitchen.

—•—

Wanna share my Nutella?

—•—

Can we fight over dinner so we can
have make-up sex for dessert?

—•—

The fact that you wash and reuse
sandwich bags is cute, not gross.

Daily Life: Bathroom

You had me at "I'll clean the bathroom."

—•—

How about I give you a facial?

Pop the Question(s)

What becomes a successful couple most? According to OkCupid, if you and your date agree on the answers to the following three questions, you stand a far greater chance of becoming a couple.

- Do you like horror movies?
- Have you ever traveled around another country alone?
- Wouldn't it be fun to chuck it all and go live on a sailboat?

I'm no artist, but I'd love to draw you a bath.

Baby, I'll clean your drain any day.

I don't even mind if you use my toothbrush.

Daily Life: Laundry

Only you can make washing
clothes look sexy.

———•◦•———

That pillow isn't the only thing
that needs fluffing around here.

———•◦•———

They call it a dryer, but it
tends to get me wet.

———•◦•———

Laundry's not the only thing
that's going for a spin in here.

———•◦•———

Maybe we should test that new
stain remover I bought.

———•◦•———

You have anything you want
to take off and throw in
with this load?

Being Parents

Accidentally knocking you up was the
best thing that ever happened to me.

I say if we don't wake at least one kid
in this house, we're not doing it right.

Be my human binky.

I can't rip those mom jeans
off you fast enough.

Your fertility-goddess
body makes me hot.

The kids are asleep . . .

I installed a lock on our bedroom door.

You make minivans sexy.

Wanna make another one?

———•·•———

When you go running with
the jogging stroller, you're the
MILF everyone talks about.

———•·•———

You're my own personal DILF.

———•·•———

There's no one else I'd rather
watch give my children things
to talk about in therapy.

Keeping the Spark Alive

Even after saying "I do," you
still make me want to do it.

———•·•———

You're always the #1 item on
my "Honey-Do" list.

———•·•———

It's not too late to follow our dreams
and start training for the Sex Olympics.

Who needs central heat
when you're around?

———•—•———

I'll warm up your side of
the bed any night.

———•—•———

It's Saturday night!

———•—•———

You know what I like
about you? My arms.

———•—•———

Why would I need porn
when I have you?

———•—•———

You make me ache in all the right places.

———•—•———

Shall we freak out the neighbors?

———•—•———

Can I try to make you
go "Squee!" again?

You must be an electrician,
because you sure know how
to keep that spark alive.

Sleeping with you makes me
want to go to the gym.

If we just met, I'd still want to
have a one-night stand.

Tip: Globally Speaking

Stumped for some original terms of endearment? Taken from a Chinese historical tale about great beauty, *chen yu luo yan* or "diving fish/swooping geese" should do the trick. In Arabic-speaking countries, *ghazal* or "gazelle" should get the heart racing. Believe it or not, *ma puce* or "my flea" is an approximation of "sweetie" in France. And in Japan, don't miss the chance to use *tamago gata no kao*—"egg with eyes."

I want you more today
than the first time we had sex in
that nightclub bathroom.

———•·•———

Why don't you turn off *Dancing
with the Stars* so I can show
you some real moves?

———•·•———

I'm wearing a matching bra and panties.

———•·•———

When you whisper like that,
I still get chills.

———•·•———

I convinced my mother to stay in a hotel.

———•·•———

Baby, if you were a hooker, it
would be at the Four Seasons.

———•·•———

Hearing your bra unsnap still
makes my stomach jump.

Growing Older

Sometimes it takes me a while to
remember that you're always right.

We can do that as much as you
desire—or until my hip gives out.

I knew you'd only improve with age.

Believe me, you'll clap every
night I take my dentures out.

Let's explore the one clear
advantage to being bedridden.

I can do without oxygen when
you're with me.

Your ears still taste like peaches.

ONLINE

When you want to stay connected

ACCORDING TO THE LATEST statistics, nearly 42 million people have tried online dating. Twenty percent of relationships begin online, and 17 percent of all married couples meet online, while only 10 percent of users abandon the online search after three months. It doesn't take a statistician to know that there are a lot of people looking for that

Tip: Be Nice

When dating online, politeness, clarity, and good grammar pay.

- Stick to English. Bad grammar and "netspeak" spelling are huge turnoffs. u feel me? ;)
- Avoid physical compliments. Calling some one hot or sexy sounds like a pickup line.
- State specific interests. Apparently, video games, zombies, tattoos, and vegetarianism are among the most popular topics.

special someone online. The jury's still out, however, as to whether digital communication has made making a love connection (or even a lusty one) easier or more complicated.

You can post all the right photos or tweak that online "personality questionnaire" to maximize your desirability percentage all you want, the fact remains: we still need to know how to talk to each other. Flirtation, even in this data-driven culture, still counts. Indeed, in an era of Tinder-swiping, gaming avatars, and 140-character limits, knowing how to flirt effectively on each different digital platform is key.

For the asocial nerd in you (or perhaps even the analog-loving Luddite)—now is the moment to rejoice. The lines contained within this chapter are designed to bring you out of your shell and engender confidence, no matter what gaming system or social network you find yourself logging into. Imagine the very language of romance merged with the cool efficiency of binary code. Isn't it time you logged on to get it on?

Tech Talking

You turn my software into hardware.

———•———

Your beauty has hacked into
the database of my heart.

———•———

I could click you all night.

———•———

You make me want
to activate my plugin.

———•———

I want to grow obsolete with you.

———•———

The feeling I get when I'm with you . . .
it's like Love 2.0.

———•———

Siri told me I should come
over and talk to you.

Want to know my password?
It's got a lot of big letters and
a few special punctuation marks.

Why don't we go back to my place
and adjust your privacy settings?

This place must be a hotspot,
because I've got full bars.

Would you like to accept my cookies?

Here are the Top 10 Reasons Why
Kissing Me Will Melt Your Heart.

I love you so much it cleared my history.

My desire for you has gone viral.

Oh baby, DM me again!

I've changed your permissions. You can now access my D: drive.

Would you mind if I uploaded a large file to your Dropbox?

I'll always love you, whether you pronounce it "gif" or "jif."

You make my hard drive solid state, baby.

I want to plug my CPU into your motherboard.

You can view my source code whenever you want.

I want to put my one in your zero.

I'd consider trading in my Mac for a PC if you went out with me.

Online Dating: Your Profile

IMHO there is no reason to check out any other profiles but mine.

———•◦•———

I've got a much better personality IRL.

———•◦•———

The first thing people usually notice about me is how generous and kind I am—and that I'm often full of shit.

Relationship Killer?

Do those who tweet have shorter relationships? Apparently, the numbers say yes. According to dating data blog OkTrends, not only do Twitter users have relationships that last an average of one month less, they masturbate a lot more, too. In fact, among some age groups, "if someone tweets every day, it's 2-to-1 that they're #ing themselves just as often." Not exactly something to chirp about, is it?

I spend a lot of time thinking
about when the lions are going to
stop playing with their food and
just eat that guy they're hugging.

———•·•———

I'm really good at macramé and ukulele.
What? No, I'm not a hipster . . .

———•·•———

I've come here to give my self-
summary and chew bubble gum—
and I'm all out of bubble gum.

———•·•———

What I'm doing with my life is reaching
out through cold and ambivalent
electronic communication for connection
and understanding. How's it working?

———•·•———

My favorite books/movies/shows/
music/food are whatever some
new list describes as the 100 best
books/movies/shows/music/food
we should all be consuming.

You can Google me if I can Google you.

My photo doesn't do me justice,
because I'm not naked.

Online Dating: Their Profile

Your profile makes me think
NSFW things.

Your smile is so bright it can
light up a chat room.

We need to clone women like you IRL.

You should message me if you've
ever watched a *Cop Rock* marathon,
because I want to know—for the
love of all that's holy, why?

YOLO—but if I come back again
I'd still Google-stalk you.

Put Your Best Profile Forward

It should come as no surprise that humans assess attractiveness within milliseconds. But that doesn't mean instant, image-first apps like Snapchat or Tinder are more successful in helping you land a date. Photos are important, but unless you're a supermodel, it pays to know how to write an effective profile as well. Experts suggest making it informative and entertaining, but concise. Brevity is appealing.

It's not fair to use a photo of a model as your profile shot.

Hey, sexy, send me more duck-face selfies!

If I told you you had a nice profile, would you hold it against me?

You, me, chemistry: NAILED IT!

———————

FWIW, your profile is perfect.

———————

Your profile is TL;DR—because
I only needed the first sentence.

———————

I like your photo. Will you marry me?

———————

I just deleted my OkCupid account.

———————

Isn't it time we took this
romance offline?

———————

If I had to choose between you and
an ice cream sundae, I'd choose
you—unless it was really hot and
I was at the beach and the sun was
going down and you were walking
by, then I'd get the sundae but
probably share some with you.

Texting

I prefer my sexting without all the "ting."

———•◦•———

Your autocorrects are making me hot.

———•◦•———

lo on pwr. come rechrg me.

———•◦•———

Remember 2 pack ur
toothbrush #sexweekend

———•◦•———

ur NSFW

———•◦•———

TMI. Keep it coming.

Gaming

Thanks to my Xbox addiction,
I've got very nimble fingers.

———•◦•———

You're so beautiful, you give
me extra hit points.

You have the biggest joystick
I've ever handled.

Oh, what amazing thumbs you have!

Do you want to dungeon my dragon?

You make me want to quit online gaming.

Social Media Sharing

Why don't you come up
and see my Tumblr?

I'll always vote up your Reddit post.

Coffee tomorrow? Color me Pinterested.

I'd like to do things you
can't post on Facebook.

I bet you get a lot of friend requests.

If you were here, I'd be
poking you for real.

I can't tell you how hot you are
in fewer than 140 characters.

I still have a crush on you,
@highschoolbabe. #tbt

#youdestroyme140charactersatatime

We follow all the same people;
clearly you're my soul mate.

Want to help me get banned
on Instagram?

You give selfies a good name.

#thelastinstagramiwillevervisit

#followme #worthit

#youreseriouslytrendingforme

I'm only wearing a #.

#youwontheinternet

You May Now Tweet the Bride

We used to ring wedding bells. Now we can just tweet—even before the wedding is over. In 2009, Dana Hanna pranked his bride by tweeting from the altar: "Standing at the altar with @TracyPage where just a second ago, she became my wife! Gotta go, time to kiss my bride. #weddingday." Tracy, just as geeky, enjoyed the joke. The Twittersphere response was mixed. Fortunately, they kept the honeymoon offline, where it belongs.

OUT & ABOUT
When the situation calls for something special

WHAT IS FLIRTATION WITHOUT
proper context? Answer: nothing
but an empty pickup line. For those
seeking to demonstrate effective
affection, there is no better context
than to cleverly acknowledge one's
location. Quite often, the road to
establishing a perfect future for
two begins with the fact that you're
both standing in the same place.

Say It, Don't Spray It

Apparently, men literally find attractive women mouthwatering. In a study at the University of Chicago, scientists tested the saliva of hetero-sexual men, then had them chat with research assistants. During the conversations, the saliva of men talking to female assistants increased, and testosterone levels leapt by 30%. The more a man tried to impress the woman, the more the testosterone jumped. Next time a guy starts to drool, take it as a compliment.

For a first time encounter, in particular, acknowledging your current whereabouts may be the only common ground the two of you share—but it's surely enough to break the ice. Mind you, this is not to say one should trot out the hoary chestnut, "What's a nice girl/boy like you doing in a place like this?" Instead, pillow talk pros know it's the details, down to the specific GPS of your meeting venue, that make the seductive difference.

Playing naive can work in your favor, even if you really do know what you're doing. As the ever-charming Alex Trebek knows, it is wisest to phrase your sweet entreaty in the form of a question. So, for your next rendezvous, try one of the provocative queries in this chapter.

Humility, or at least a winking nod to it, can be catnip to a successful conversation. Players are advised to never assume you know more than your (future) partner. Who knows, that cute young thing you bumped into at the farmer's market just might be a three-star chef.

Dog Park

What a beautiful tail.

———•—•———

Seeing you here, I get why all
those tongues are hanging out.

———•—•———

You're so soft—so gentle—so sweet.
Now, tell me, how's your pooch doing?

———•—•———

You always know just where to scratch.

———•—•———

@dogparkbabe You said fetch,
now where do I bring the
bone? #tailwaggin

———•—•———

Dogs know how to play
rough. What about you?

———•—•———

I love it when you do that shake.

Oh, your filthy paws!

———•◆•———

I could watch that tail wag all day.

———•◆•———

Smart dog; I'd follow you home, too.

School

Feel like going for extra credit?

———•◆•———

I'm really cheering just for you.

———•◆•———

I'll see you in detention
tonight—you bad, bad boy.

———•◆•———

Wanna get together and cram?

———•◆•———

So, professor, how would you grade
my performance this time?

All this towel-snapping and butt-slapping can only mean one thing.

———•———

Beat my eraser—hard.

Gym

Sorry for staring—are you
exercising your kegels?

———•———

Let's work out how
we're going to see each other
someplace more private.

———•———

You've clearly got the form down—can
you show me how that machine works?

———•———

If you come home with me, you
won't need the gym anymore.

———•———

How many years did it take
you to get glutes like that?

I can't lift weights
around you; you always
make me lose count.

·——•◆•——·

Your form is perfect
on that warrior pose. Are
you a yoga teacher?

·——•◆•——·

Can you spot me while I do
this headstand?

The Heat of the Night

What makes a city romantic? Using data based
on what its citizens buy online, Amazon claims
the friskiest clicking belongs to San Antonio,
TX; Seattle, WA; and Knoxville, TN, where Barry
White albums, relationship books, and "sexual
wellness" products are bought by the virtual
cartload. New York City and El Monte, CA, are
frosty customers by comparison—though perhaps it's because they've dropped their laptops
to enjoy a candlelit dinner instead.

How do you make that pose
look so effortless?

———————

Where did you learn to
chant like that, India?

———————

The best spot in yoga is right behind you.

Market

It looks like I picked the right
checkout line.

———————

I've always wondered what to do with
leeks. What do *you* do with them?

———————

That vitamin is clearly working for
you. How long have you been using it?

———————

From the looks of your cart,
and the tone of your abs, you
must be on the paleo diet.

Can you tell if these melons are ripe?

Can you help me find the honey?

Coffee House

Do you have sugar, or can you just smile at my coffee until it's sweet?

I could watch you steam milk all day.

I like my mochaccino like I like my men: tall, covered with whipped cream and cocoa, with just a hint of vanilla.

Can I warm that up for you?

Would two fingers worth be enough room for cream?

I have to admit I'm a little jealous of your laptop.

A Rose by Any Other Name

Historically, a little musk was the way to a suitor's heart. In Elizabethan England, a maiden might give her beau an apple slice she'd kept under her armpit. Traditional Balkan dancing includes a handkerchief from a man's pit waved under the noses of females. And a 2009 *The Journal of Neuroscience* study shows why: Women can sniff out sexual sweat, so be prepared when you give out that armpit hanky.

Nightclub

Is that a fertility dance you're doing?
'Cause it's totally working on me.

———

If I buy you a drink, will you
buy me breakfast?

———

You'll probably look good
even when I'm sober.

Is it the wine or you making
me feel dizzy?

———•———

This happy hour would be better
if your clothing was half-off.

Pot Shop

Whoa. That's the same ultra-potent
strain I was going to pick!

———•———

Let's make like love muffins
and get totally baked.

———•———

There's nothing here I would wrap my
lips around and smoke more than you.

———•———

Just seeing you in here gets me high.

———•———

You are totally blazing.

———•———

You put the stick in my sticky-icky-icky.

I could get addicted to you.

———•———

You light up my life—among
other groovy things.

———•———

You truly are smoking hot.

Behind Bars

I wouldn't trade what we have for
anything in the world—except
maybe a few packs of smokes.

———•———

I remember the first time you
smuggled your way into my heart.

———•———

You're the best thing that ever
happened to D-Block.

———•———

Do you like piña coladas and
long walks on the yard?

Let's break these chains that bind us!

Other than four feet of
reinforced concrete, nothing
can keep us from our love.

I feel so solitary without you here.

You're so turned on—you totally want
to shiv me right now, don't you?

Care for a little bedtime reading? I just
got a new tatt with your name on it.

Tonight, make like the
warden and set me free.

You wear your twenty years to life well.

Damn, I dropped the soap
again. Mind backing me up?

Military

Is that a gun in your hand, soldier,
or are you just happy to see me?

All we need
is a good foxhole
and some candlelight.

Come closer
if you really want to learn
how I earned my stripes.

One look at you and they knew
why I recruited you.

You always have permission
to board me, sailor.

Whaddya say
we haul out the big guns?

We begin banging
in five minutes.

Show me how you swab
that poop deck again.

You make every part of me want
to stand stiffly at attention.

Tip: Look Out! Now Kiss Me

The Schachter-Singer theory is the ultimate
wingman: Put someone in a dangerous
situation that produces the same symptoms
as physical attraction (racing heart, sweaty
palms, rapid breathing) and he or she just
might think it's you acting as stimuli. Even
running in place can produce the same effect.
So whether it's working out, riding a roller
coaster, or seeing a scary film, do your best to
get that special someone's heart pounding.

Outdoor Sports & Recreation

It's nearly impossible to make bike shorts look good—but you do.

———•———

You always give my ride a kickstand, baby.

———•———

My nickname is "The Home Run King," but I never play baseball.

———•———

You could help me make sure that someone scores tonight.

———•———

Will you give me mouth-to-mouth after the 5K?

———•———

I'm always in the deep end when you're around.

———•———

I'd love to help you improve your stroke.

Cultural Events

You make it so even the
ballet doesn't suck.

Going to a museum with you makes
abstract expressionist work make sense.

You're the only priceless work
of art in this place.

I don't even notice that the guy
next to me is snoring when I go
to the symphony with you.

You look like someone who
would know where the erotica
section of this bookstore is.

If you like my caesura
you'll love my sestet.

FAMOUS CHARM

When you want to leave it up to the experts

SEDUCTION IS A TRICKY BUSINESS. And for many, expressing one's feelings is even harder. And yet few of us can go through life without giving either one a shot. Practice makes perfect, of course, and since sweet nothings are meant to accomplish both difficult tasks, why not begin your training by borrowing from the best?

When Stars Align

It turns out the next best thing to being in love is watching two people in a film do it . . . fall in love, that is. Neuropsychologist Dr. David Lewis says that when we see stars kiss onscreen, our brain's mirror neurons start firing. "Each person mistakenly attributes a part of the adrenaline buzz produced by the film to the presence of their partner." So the next time you watch *The Notebook*, you'll know why you think the guy near you is Ryan Gosling.

For centuries, philosophers and poets have put the complex human emotions of love, lust, and longing into concise, memorable quotations that ring true. The movie industry, too, when it is not satisfying the global need for well-muscled action flicks or superhero adventures, specializes in the craft of the romantic comedy. Popular songs offer up chapter and verse to school you in your pursuit of *l'amour*, and even television has provided some classic heart-stopping moments of deathless romantic dialogue. Consider this chapter a key reference text in your seduction lesson plan.

Representing a greatest-hits collection of amorous declarations and alluring observations, the following pages of time-tested pillow talk are meant to inspire the idealistic cupid hiding in all of us. Harness their inspiring power and put them to good use. Plus, these well-composed quips of the romantically well-spoken are royalty-free. So please, feel free to speak them with abandon.

Television

"Before I met you the sun was like a yellow grape. But now, it look like fire in the sky. Why? Because you light a fire inside me." —Uzo Aduba as Suzanne "Crazy Eyes" Warren in *Orange is the New Black*

"That thing you did with your mouth—is that what lords do to their ladies in the south?" —Rose Leslie as Ygritte in *Game of Thrones*

"When I saw you sleeping there, I thought, I couldn't imagine not seeing you there every morning." —Jon Hamm as Don Draper in *Mad Men*

"Pick *me*. Choose *me*. Love *me*." —Ellen Pompeo as Meredith in *Grey's Anatomy*

"You're all I need. I love you and I like you." —Amy Poehler as Leslie Knope in *Parks and Recreation*

"The only thing that matters is that you make me happier than I ever thought I could be. And if you let me, I will spend the rest of my life trying to make you feel the same way." —Matthew Perry as Chandler in *Friends*

"I do feel used, and played, and lied to, but I also feel good. Two minutes with you, and I feel good." —Damian Lewis as Brody in *Homeland*

"We can't stop. I can't. You're the most important person in my life. I can't just stop. Can you?" —Tony Goldwyn as President Fitzgerald Grant in *Scandal*

Film

"I'm scared of walking out of this room and never feeling the rest of my whole life the way I feel when I'm with you." —Jennifer Grey as Baby in *Dirty Dancing*

"You make me wanna be a better man." —Jack Nicholson as Melvin in *As Good as It Gets*

"You gotta be kiddin' me. All this time, that's what I've been missin'? Let's do it again." —Rachel McAdams as Allie in *The Notebook*

"You should be kissed, and often, and by someone who knows how." —Clark Gable as Rhett in *Gone with the Wind*

"I have crossed oceans of time to find you." —Gary Oldman as Dracula in *Bram Stoker's Dracula*

"To me, you are perfect." —Andrew Lincoln as Mark in *Love Actually*

"There's a shortage of perfect breasts in this world. It would be a pity to damage yours." —Cary Elwes as Westley in *The Princess Bride*

"I'm also just a girl, standing in front of a boy, asking him to love her." —Julia Roberts as Anna in *Notting Hill*

Lusty Lit

Embarrassed to prefer the pillow talk you find between the pages of a book? You're hardly alone. According to the Romance Writers of America website, romance novels have the largest share of the consumer market, with more than a billion dollars in sales annually. E-books have made them even more popular. Offering plenty of sexual repartee, romance novels aren't bad places to pick up your own sweet nothings.

"If you won't sleep with me this time I want you to know that you can call me up anytime you want and we'll make some kind of an arrangement." —Ann Bancroft as Mrs. Robinson in *The Graduate*

———◆———

"I was hoping you'd give me a bath. I'm very, very dirty." —Mena Suvari as Angela in *American Beauty*

———◆———

"I've got a funny sensation in my toes, like someone was barbecuing them over a slow flame." —Tony Curtis as Joe in *Some Like It Hot*

———◆———

"Now lick your lips. Again ... again." —Colin Firth as Johannes in *Girl with a Pearl Earring*

———◆———

"Mac could make Valerie feel very, very good." —Jeff Goldblum as Mac in *Earth Girls Are Easy*

"I wish I knew how to quit you." —Jake Gyllenhaal as Jack in *Brokeback Mountain*

"I came here tonight because when you realize you want to start the rest of your life with somebody, you want the rest of your life to start as soon as possible." —Billy Crystal as Harry in *When Harry Met Sally*

"Let's try it again, only this time I'm going to stick my tongue in your mouth. And when I do that, I want you to massage my tongue with yours. And that's what first base is." —Sarah Michelle Gellar as Kathryn in *Cruel Intentions*

"What do you want? You want the moon? Just say the word and I'll throw a lasso around it and pull it down." —James Stewart as George in *It's a Wonderful Life*

Legendary TMI

It's good that celebrity pillow talk doesn't often become public, since the few conversations that surface are cringe-worthy. In a call with his lover Camilla Parker Bowles, Prince Charles crooned, "I'll just live inside your trousers." Mark Sanford, governor of South Carolina, praised his mistress' tan lines, the curves of her hips, and "the erotic beauty of you holding yourself (or two magnificent parts of yourself) in the faded glow of night's light."

"I am unhappy because I want you. Because my mind is seized on you and can think of nothing else. This is how I suffer. I'm sick with longing. I don't eat. I don't sleep. So if you've come with no feeling for me, then go."
—Harvey Keitel as George in *The Piano*

"I love you. You complete me." —Tom Cruise as Jerry in *Jerry Maguire*

"Why don't we skip dinner altogether and go straight to dessert?" —Jonathan Rhys Meyers as James in *From Paris with Love*

<hr/>

"I promise, I'll come back for you. I promise, I'll never leave you." —Ralph Fiennes as Count Laszlo in *The English Patient*

Literature

"I have little left in myself—I must have you. The world may laugh—may call me absurd, selfish—but it does not signify. My very soul demands you: it will be satisfied: or it will take deadly vengeance on its frame." —Charlotte Brontë, *Jane Eyre*

<hr/>

"Every time you move tomorrow, I want you to be reminded that I've been here. Only me. You are mine." —E L James, *Fifty Shades of Grey*

"How do I love thee? Let me count the ways. / I love thee to the depth and breadth and height / My soul can reach, when feeling out of sight . . . "
—Elizabeth Barrett Browning, *Sonnets from the Portuguese, Sonnet 43*

"Then move not, while my prayer's effect I take. Thus from my lips, by yours, my sin is purged." —William Shakespeare, *Romeo and Juliet*

"I want to do with you what spring does with the cherry trees." —Pablo Neruda, *Twenty Love Poems and a Song of Despair*

"It would be a privilege to have my heart broken by you." —John Green, *The Fault in Our Stars*

"When are you sailing so I can meet you at the the dock with champagne?" —Robert Lowell, *Words in Air*

Music

"Baby, kiss me / Before they turn the lights out." —Beyoncé, "XO"

"Lovin' you is easy 'cause you're beautiful / Makin' love with you is all I wanna do / Lovin' you is more than just a dream come true / And everything that I do is out of lovin' you." —Minnie Riperton, "Lovin' You"

"And givin' yourself to me can never be wrong / If the love is true." —Marvin Gaye, "Let's Get It On"

"Whenever you're near / I hear a symphony." —The Supremes, "I Hear a Symphony"

"I don't make the kind of love that's only for a minute / I'll be inside of you as long as you want me in it." —Barry White, "I Only Want to Be with You"

"I knew I loved you before I met you /
I think I dreamed you into life."
—Savage Garden, "I Knew I Loved You"

"Have I told you lately that I love you? /
Have I told you there's no one else
above you?" —Van Morrison, "Have
I Told You Lately That I Love You"

"Voulez-vouz coucher avec moi, ce soir?"
—Patti LaBelle, "Lady Marmalade"

"Ooooh, I don't wanna see you be no
fool / What I'm teachin' you tonight /
Boy, you'll never learn it in school,
oh, no." —Sylvia, "Pillow Talk"

"I want to love you, feel you / Wrap
myself around you / I want to squeeze
you, please you / I just can't get enough."
—The Pointer Sisters, "I'm So Excited"

"Your body is a wonderland. / Your body is a wonder (I'll use my hands)." —John Mayer, "Your Body is a Wonderland"

"Rubbin' sticks and stones together makes the sparks ignite / And the thought of lovin' you is getting so exciting." —Starland Vocal Band, "Afternoon Delight"

Classical Cussing

Naughty language in popular culture isn't new. A raunchy translation of Aristophanes' *Lysistrata* includes such slang as "ball," used as a verb, and Catullus was a big fan of a slur that rhymes with trick. In *The Canterbury Tales*, Chaucer used the cruder words for derriere, poop, piddle, and female anatomy (charmingly spelled with a "qu"). Shakespeare and Joyce had fun with tongue-in-cheek swearing like "See you in tea" and "If you see kay" (say them aloud).

"I thank the gods of Groupon for landing us in these same ten yoga classes."